Contents

Author: .... **Error! Bookmark not defined.**

Disclaimer 4

Review of the Story 6

"Thomas's Magical Adventure in the Maldives" 9

The End. 25

"Thomas Magical Adventure in the Maldives"

Author
Ibrahim Ilyas

Disclaimer

Copyright © 2023 by Ibrahim Ilyas, All rights reserved.

No part of this story may be reproduced, stored, or transmitted in any form or by any means, electronic, mechanical, photocopying, recording, or otherwise, without prior written permission of the author.

Review of the Story

This is a great story about a young boy named Thomas who goes on a family holiday trip to the Maldives. The story does a great job of describing the stunning beauty of the Maldives and the wonderful experiences that Thomas and his family had while there. From going on a boat tour and seeing the coral reefs and the vibrant colors of the fish, to snorkeling and seeing the majestic whale sharks, to exploring a hidden lagoon with an amazing waterfall, to see the local wildlife,

Thomas and his family had an amazing time and lots of wonderful experiences. The story is well-written and engaging, and the author does a great job of conveying the beauty and wonder of the Maldives. All in all, this is a wonderful story that any child would enjoy.

"Thomas Magical Adventure in the Maldives"

Once upon a time, there lived a little boy named Thomas who loved to explore and go on adventures. His family was planning a holiday trip to the Maldives, and Thomas was so excited to discover all the beautiful sights the island had to offer.

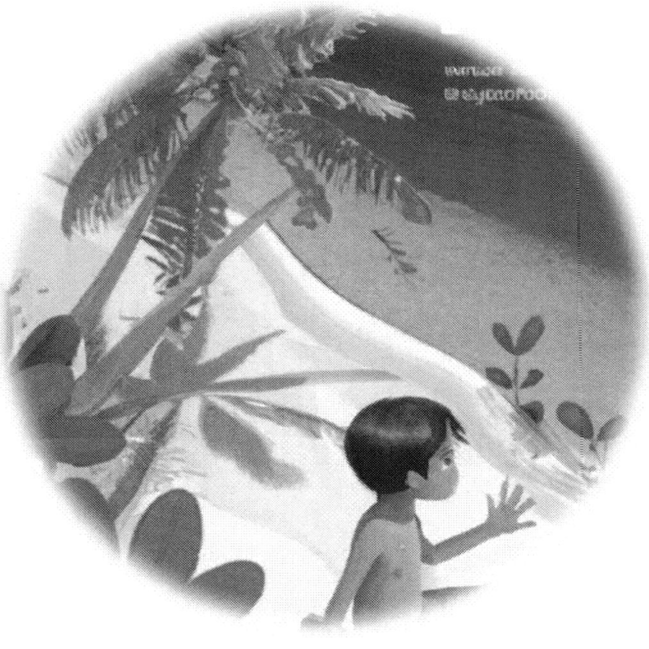

When Thomas and his family arrived in the Maldives, they were amazed by its natural beauty. The air was so fresh and the waters so blue, it was like being in a paradise. Thomas and his family decided to go on a boat tour to explore the islands and experience the beauty of the Maldives.

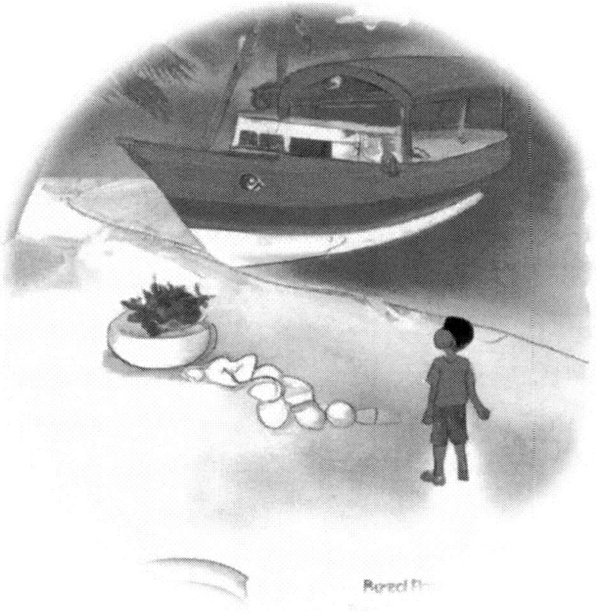

The boat tour went around the islands, and Thomas was able to see the amazing coral reefs and the vibrant colors of the fish that swam in the sea. He even spotted a few dolphins jumping in the water. Thomas was absolutely in awe of the beauty of the Maldives.

The tour then took them to a spot where the guides said they could see whale sharks. Thomas was so excited to see these majestic creatures. When they arrived, the guides told them to be very quiet and still, so as not to disturb the whale sharks.

Thomas and his family put on their snorkeling gear and jumped into the water. At first, Thomas was a bit scared, but soon he felt mesmerized by the beauty of the underwater world. He watched as the whale sharks gracefully swam around him, their giant bodies gliding through the water. Thomas was so amazed by the experience, he couldn't believe his eyes.

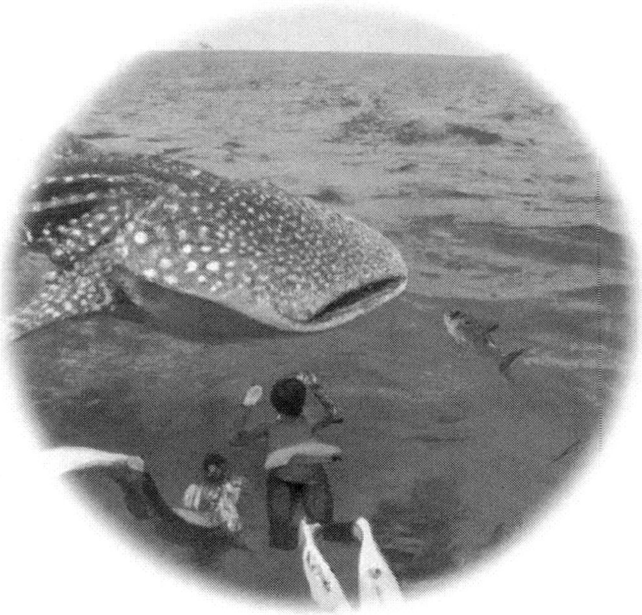

After the whale shark experience, Thomas and his family continued their tour around the islands. They visited a local village and went on a wonderful hike through the jungle. They even got to explore a hidden lagoon with an amazing waterfall.

At the end of the day, Thomas and his family returned to their resort and enjoyed a delicious dinner and some much-needed rest. Thomas was so excited to tell his friends and family back home all about his amazing adventure in the Maldives.

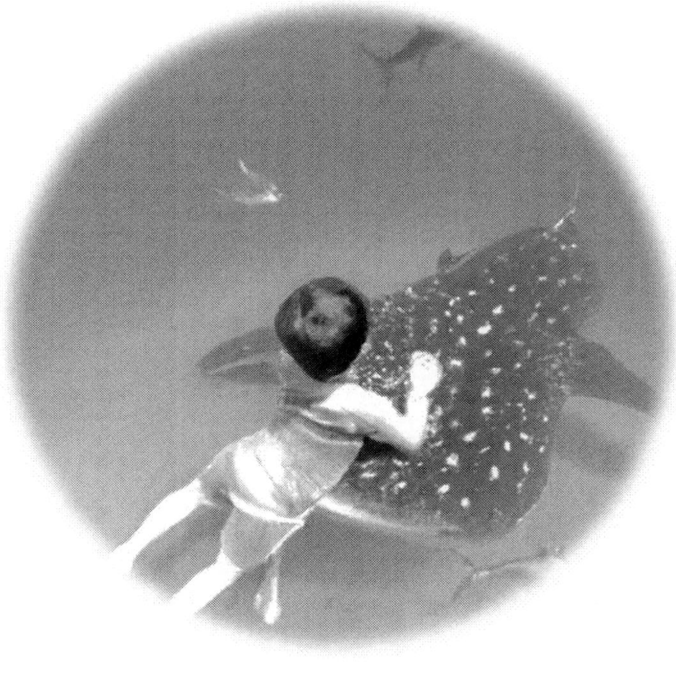

The next morning, Thomas and his family got up early to go on one last excursion. They took a speedboat out to a nearby island, and Thomas was amazed by the gorgeous views of the ocean. He also got to see some of the local wildlife, including some beautiful birds and a few dolphins.

When they arrived on the island, Thomas and his family got to go on an incredible snorkeling adventure. Thomas was amazed by the colorful coral reefs and the fish that swam around him. He even got to see some sea turtles and a few friendly dolphins.

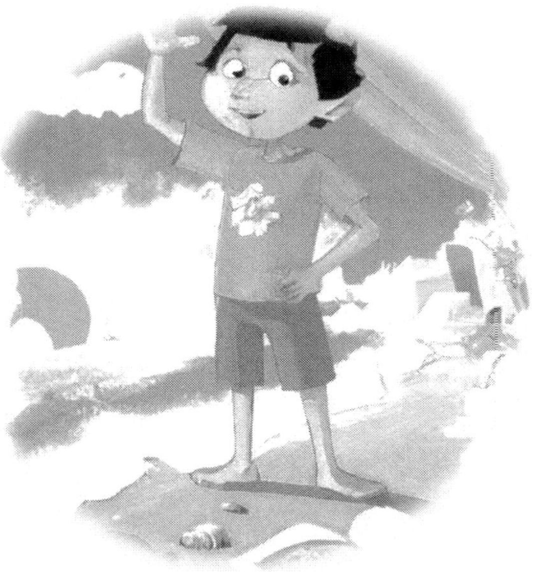

At the end of the day, Thomas and his family returned to their resort, exhausted and happy. Thomas was so glad he had gotten to experience the Maldives. He couldn't wait to go back one day and explore even more of the beauty and wonders of the Maldives.

The next morning, Thomas and his family got up early to catch their flight back home. As they left, Thomas looked back and waved goodbye to the beautiful Maldives. He knew he would never forget the amazing experience he had there.

The End.